The
Road to
Cleethorpes Pier

Cleethorpes Pier, August 2019

The Road to Cleethorpes Pier

MARGARET ROYALL

A Memoir in Prose and Verse

Crumps Barn Studio

In memory of my beloved husband, Garry Richard Royall (1942–1998) and my dear friend Judith Marion Howitt, née Smalley (1944–1999). They have left me with a massive hole in my life but also wonderful memories, which can never be erased

Crumps Barn Studio LLP
Crumps Barn, Syde, Cheltenham GL53 9PN
www.crumpsbarnstudio.co.uk

Copyright © Margaret Royall 2020

First printed 2020

The right of Margaret Royall to be identified as the author of this work has been asserted by her in accordance with the Copyright, Designs and Patents Act 1988.

All rights reserved. No part of this publication may be reproduced, stored in a retrieval system, or transmitted in any form or by any means, electronic, mechanical, photocopying, recording or otherwise, without the prior permission of the copyright owner.

Cover design by Lorna Gray © Crumps Barn Studio
Cover photograph © Margaret Royall
Photographic plates © Margaret Royall

ISBN 978-1-9998705-7-7

A note from the author

My memoir is told through a mix of poetry and prose and I have chosen this deliberately. I love the Japanese poetry forms of Haiku and Haibun and have chosen to use the latter, adapting it to align with western tastes and to reflect my writing style.

Haibun is a prosimetric literary form originating in Japan, combining prose and haiku (or in this case contemporary poetry). The range of haibun is broad and frequently includes autobiography, diary, essay, prose poem, short story and travel journal.

A very precious, very old photo of my paternal grandmother, Jessie Browning (née Croft; front row, centre), and her many sisters and brother with her parents (my great grandparents). They were known as the family of poets, as Jessie married a Browning, one sister a Thackeray and another sister a Burns!

Interestingly, many of the wider family were writers, including my dad, his cousin and my son Simon. My mum (though not a Browning) won a national sonnet competition – her entry and accompanying illustration have sadly been lost, but it was 'Ode to Newport Arch', a Roman archway still surviving in Lincoln.

Contents

Where It All Began	3
A Seaside Childhood	*7*
The Road to Cleethorpes Pier	*11*
My Parents	13
On The Beach With Michael	*17*
The Fitties	*19*
Christmas at Sherburn Street	*21*
Methodist Sunday School 1948	29
The 'Gas(light) Chamber'	*35*
Sunday Afternoons on the Wolds	*39*
Celebrating Harvest Festival	42
Autumn Blows In	*43*
My imaginary friends	47
Grandma and Granddad Browning	*51*
Lady with Lavender Aura	*53*

Nanny Buttle's Pork Chops	*57*
Great Aunts Jessie and Nellie	*59*
Visits to Louth and the nearby Hubbards Hills	63
Bursar County Primary Junior School, Cleethorpes	65
The Episode with the Psalm and the Bishop	*69*
More About My Parents	71
Washday Wednesdays	*75*
Fish and Chips	*77*
Tea in Guy and Smith's Cafe	*79*
To London by Steam Train	81
The Clementina Clee Years: Life at Grammar School	85
Clementina Clees	*89*
M J B	*91*
My Friend Ann	93
My First Taste of Privilege	*94*
An Unusual Friendship	*95*
Her Family Home	*96*
Rent Collection in the Rolls Royce	*97*
Awkward Moments in the Royal Albert Hall, London	99
The Ferry Across the Humber	105
On Board a Grimsby Trawler	108

A Summer Week in Alford	111
'Johnny, Remember Me'	*113*
Tasting a Different Culture	117
The Aidan's Maidens Years: Life at Durham University	125
My Year In Germany	130
Vorsprung Durch Technik	*131*
My Year at Cambridge University	133
Arrival of the Queen of Sheba	*137*
Twenty Years On	*141*
Teetotalism	147
Hope is a Rainbow	*149*
The Time Thief	*151*
The Verdict	*153*
Cleethorpes: A Brief Overview	157
A Place to Grow Strong Bones	*159*
Love Calls Me Home	*161*

My parents on their wedding day outside Mill Road Methodist Church, Cleethorpes

Where It All Began

I was born on 10th September 1944 at the Croft Baker Maternity Home in Cleethorpes, Lincolnshire, the first-born child of Edmund Joseph Browning and Kathleen Browning (née Buttle), both Cleethorpes residents.

My father was a gentleman's outfitter, having served his apprenticeship in the gent's department of a thriving Grimsby department store, Lawson and Stockdale's. My mother had previously worked in the china department of another highly respected Grimsby department store, Guy and Smith's. I was their only child, which saddened me, as I would have loved to have had siblings to play with.

Readers may have heard of the town Cleethorpes, as it has often been the butt of comedians' jokes. Or they may have heard of its reputation as a windy, often chilly seaside resort. It lies on the Lincolnshire coast at the mouth of the River Humber estuary, where it joins the North Sea – which explains why the tide comes in and out of the resort and is sometimes nowhere to be seen at all!

There has been much redevelopment in recent decades and many of the features I knew and loved as a child have gone – e.g. the Winter Gardens, the Bathing Pool. However, there is still a pier, a promenade, a boating lake, a scaled-down display of illuminations and of course the vast beach area which was the go-to resort when I was a child for day-trippers and vacationers from the Midlands and Yorkshire industrial towns.

We lived at 14 Sherburn Street in a semi-detached, rented bungalow in a residential part of the town with easy access to the town centre, shops and beach. Much of the furniture was utility ware. There were two bedrooms, a kitchen area which we called the scullery, which strangely housed a screened off cubicle with our only toilet. Beside this was a storage room referred to as 'the glory hole', since a variety of household equipment as well as bags of coke and coal were stored there. Also off the kitchen was a huge pantry with shelving and a meat safe (we had no fridge until I was in my teens).

We had a living room, a 'front' room (used on special occasions or when we had visitors), and a bathroom with bath and washbasin. There was a small front garden and a larger rear garden containing the shell of a former concrete air-raid shelter. To the side of the house was a broad passageway known as the 'eightfoot', and at the far end was a repair garage run by Mr. Whaley, a cheerful car mechanic.

My parents never owned their own home and lived very frugally by today's standards. I recall many problems with property repairs and great upheaval when dry rot was discovered and had to be eliminated. These were the post-war years with rationing still in place and our diet and lifestyle, to which I refer at various points, were very simple indeed. Yet I never felt deprived, as this was all I knew. I counted myself lucky to be raised in a loving home by loving parents, who were very proud of me. I wanted for nothing.

Historical note:
Utility furniture was furniture produced in the United Kingdom during and just after World War II, under a Government scheme which was designed to cope with shortages of raw materials and rationing of consumption. Introduced in 1942, the Utility Furniture Scheme continued into post-war austerity and lasted until 1952.

Me and my friend Michael at the beach, aged 3

A Seaside Childhood

I never missed my childhood home
until the tide stopped rolling in and
ochre sand no longer crunched between my toes

That Siberian wind numbing body and soul,
collars up, heads bent on the mile-long prom
between the Winter Gardens and the pier.

The boy with the leaking boot grinning down,
the dish plotting to elope with the spoon
and the man in the moon winking cheekily at passers-by

Never serious rivals to the Blackpool lights
but we always did the rounds, pretended to be
awe-struck, ate fish and chips out of newspaper.

In Summer we squelched across the mud
for what seemed like miles, sliding over sandbanks,
seeking the grey embrace of the North Sea,

Always watching out for the turn of the tide,
unpredictable, quick to swamp the creak behind us –
never forgetting that atrocious riding school tragedy

In the sultry haze of mid Summer I miss those familiar things ...
Licking ice lollies on the Brighton Slipway,
wrestling with sticks of tooth-breaking Cleethorpes rock

We would watch the patient donkeys schlepping
up and down the beach, children building sandcastles,
old men draped over railings, gazing wistfully out to sea

Seagulls screeching as they wheeled and dive-bombed trippers,
rollers crashing against the brine-soaked breakwaters.
Strange how much you miss things once they're gone!

Historical note:
In 1969 a thick fog descended without warning on a group of children having their first riding lesson on the beach. It is thought they became disorientated and instead of turning back for home walked straight out to sea. With the tide coming in around them they perished. The tragedy rocked the town and has never been forgotten.

On Cleethorpes Beach with my mum in 1948

The Road to Cleethorpes Pier

Each grain of sand a shiver down my spine,
a memory harvested from fields of youth,
stowed safely in the vaults of passing time

The sand streams silently through open fingers,
rewinding spools of childhood innocence,
time's smile a crooked barb that cuts too deep

The vault was locked, keys hidden away, for fear
the salted wounds might burst their skin again
and memories' spilt blood poison the heart

The sandy trail leads back to Cleethorpes pier
and tides that washed the slate clean every day,
five miles of golden sand – a postcard whim

And yet I long to open up the vault,
to face the memories, good and bad once more …
to count each grain then cast it to the wind

My parents as I always remember them

My Parents

My mother and father were a devoutly Methodist couple, working tirelessly for their local chapel, in those days called Mill Road Methodist Chapel (now rebuilt and the name changed to St Andrew's Methodist Chapel). I mention this fact, as it has great relevance for my childhood and adolescence, and features frequently in this memoir – Methodism reigned supreme in Lincolnshire and regular attendance at Sunday School and chapel was the norm in the area in the 1940s and 1950s.

My parents in fact met through the church, married there and I was baptised there as Margaret Jean Browning. They devoted their lives to service at Mill Road Chapel – my father as Captain of the Boys' Brigade, my mother as Captain of its junior section, The Lifebuoys. You could compare the Boys' Brigade and Lifebuoys to the probably better-known Scout and Cub movement. There was a similar movement for girls called in my day The Girls' Life Brigade (now simply The Girls' Brigade) to which I naturally belonged from the age of six.

My father's sister, Jessie May, was also leader of the Primary Section of Mill Road Sunday School and it was taken as read that I would eventually become a Sunday School teacher myself.

In addition my father was a lay preacher and sometimes took me with him on a Sunday morning to outlying village chapels where he was preaching. Sometimes the congregation would only comprise one or two farmers and we would be invited back to lunch at their farmhouse. Often my dad had to play the organ for the hymns and I would occasionally need to pump it!

This was the background into which I was born and explains the predominance of church-related memories (although I hasten to add that they are not all serious, some being hopefully more amusing). I just wanted to explain that it was pretty much a *fait accompli* that my formative years would be greatly influenced by the church.

Historical note:
Lincolnshire was the birth place of the founders of Methodism, John Wesley and his brother Charles, so at that time the area was a stronghold of Methodism and it exerted great influence over the population.

Aged 18 months with a doll's pram

*Aged 3 with Michael, and his mum
and younger brother*

On The Beach With Michael

Glossary:
Meggies – folk originating from Cleethorpes. The origin of the term is disputed.
Tansad – a type of pushchair with adjustable footboard in use in the 1940s/50s. Tansad became a generic name for a baby buggy

The adverts for Cleethorpes boasted
five miles of glorious golden sand –
no mention of the biting east wind!

The Meggies were always a hardy bunch –
a daily dose of mind-numbing fresh air
an absolute must for the health-conscious locals.

My mum and her friends believed in bracing walks.
She would push me in the old Tansad along the Kingsway –
fine when I didn't have to share it with Michael

Oh how I hated him, loud, impatient, whiny,
sharing the pram with *a boy* was humiliating.
The only recompense a choc-ice at the end,

bought from Mr Oliphant's open-all-hours shop,
crammed with buckets, spades and kiss-me-quick hats,
exuding cheerful optimism on the sea-front

Familiarity breeds contempt, they say. How true!
It is only now, living as I do in a landlocked place,
that I find myself craving the wildness of that seashore

The Fitties

> Humberston Fitties is an historic location close to the Victorian resort of Cleethorpes. Fitties is a local word meaning 'salt marsh'. The Fitties comprises 320 individual chalets set back from roads and dirt tracks, close to sand dunes and the Fitties beach. In 1995 it was declared a conservation area.

Maybe it was the precursor to Butlins?
Difficult to imagine how strangers
might view this seaside sprawl.

A holiday camp of sorts,
yet no two chalets the same;
some rough-hewn, in need of repair,
some primped and preened
with manicured lawns,
gnomes in the garden
and white picket fences.
We laughed at the comical names:
Dunroamin' Linga Longa or Pooh Corner.

Once A level exams were over
we headed there to relax and chill –
a gaggle of innocent virgins,
shocked by the sight of a
naked man in the dunes
towelling himself dry after a swim!

Carefree days spent sunbathing,
eating cockles and shrimps out of paper bags.
At school assiduous pupils, top of the class,
but pretty clueless about the big wide world
beyond the reach of academia.

Life was about to change for ever
breathing in for the very first time
the heady air of independence, rebellion,
a taste of future freedom in the fullness of time.

Christmas at Sherburn Street

Mock crab, as made by my gran, was a mixture of melted cheese, cooked tomatoes and vinegar beaten into a paste to spread hot on toast or use as a cold sandwich filling. Other versions I have found online mention the inclusion of egg. It supposedly looked like a crab paste.

T'was the night before Christmas
our small home was filled
with happy excitement
and Christmas goodwill.
My parents assured me
Santa came through the door,
so they left it ajar
with his treats on the floor.
He could wipe his big boots
caked with mud from the sleigh,
have his mince pie and cake
and then go on his way

Sleep never came quickly
so I stayed wide awake,
so anxious to catch him
eating mince pie and cake!
I wanted to see
if he had a white beard
and a thick, fur-lined red coat,
but what I most feared
was that Daddy might come
and lock up the front door,
so I kept an eye open
(It had happened before!)

All night I would call
to my parents asleep
"Has he been yet with presents?
Can I take a quick peep?"
By six they would give in,
allow me to snuggle
in bed with them both
in a family cuddle.
I was handed a stocking
with presents galore;

it seemed like a hundred,
well, twenty or more!
I squealed with delight
as I opened each gift,
ripping off pretty paper,
my young hands so swift…
The biggest and best gift
was set well aside,
A teddy or new doll,
blue eyes open wide

It was church after breakfast
with carols round the tree
then Christmas lunch beckoned,
a favourite for me was
roast chicken and trimmings
with stuffing made from bread.
I loathed Christmas pud
so had Yorkshire instead,
all smothered in treacle,
a golden, gooey treat,
much nicer than suet
and horrid mince meat!

Teatime was always
a Browning affair
in Whites Road at Grandma
and Grandad's house; there
was roast ham, tomatoes
and mock crab on toast,
then pear halves, evap milk,
best food they could boast.
More presents to open
and carols to sing,
a huge fir tree decked
with Victorian things,
and candles alight
on the end of each bough,
with angel chimes tinkling
away down below

A fairytale time
that came round once a year …
When the big day was over
I'd shed a few tears.
Without sleep that night
and so much in my head,
a tired little child
would go early to bed

Sometimes on Boxing Day
soon after lunch
we'd climb in our Austin 7
to follow the hunt.
The car had no heating
so rugs were the thing
that staved off the cold
when neatly tucked in,

and often hot water bottles
placed on our feet,
and flasks of hot soup
with cheese butties to eat.
We headed for Brocklesby,
hoping to see
the huntsmen and hounds,
a real thrill for me

Then later the great aunts
came round to take tea
with jelly, ice-cream and
blancmange, all wobbly;
and chocolate cake, Christmas cake,
egg custard tarts,
my mum baked such treats
as would melt children's hearts

The TV showed pantomime,
same boring themes,
but for aunts with no TV
it captured their dreams.
They opened their presents
with long ooohs and aaahs,
gave flowers to my mum
which we put in a vase

Then Christmas was over
and all that good cheer
was packed away safely
until the next year.
I so loved those times
filled with love, hope and joy,
their magic long cherished
by each girl and boy.

With Dad, Grandma Browning and Jessie in 1952

A church Summer Garden Party in 1952, where the theme was Nursery Rhyme Land. I'm on the top row, 3rd from right and my best friend Judith is on the same row, 3rd from left.

My character was Little Miss Muffet and Judith's was Mary Mary Quite Contrary.

Methodist Sunday School 1948

'Judith's got her foot stuck in the chair!' yelled a cheeky eight year old with a mischievous grin, rudely interrupting the celebrations in full flow.

Hymn books crashed to the ground, collection plates went flying, parents leapt to their feet ('Whose child was it?'), piercing howl from child in question, gasps of horror, pandemonium!

'Try pulling your foot back through, dear,' from the Nursery Leader trying to be practical.

'Can't, can't!' The child in question howled louder, embarrassed onlookers strained to see what the kerfuffle was about.

A red-faced father rushed forward and seized his three year old, foot still through chair and carried her off the platform and out of the chapel, still howling. As her best friend I was concerned and decided I too wanted to be removed.

No, this was not a scene from an infant nativity play, not an end of term concert; just the annual Sunday School Anniversary celebrations in Mill Road Methodist Chapel.

Such pent up excitement, such stress for the young performers. Something unexpected happened every year, fuelling stories for years to come. One year John Broughton was sick all over the carpet, one year the soloist was so overcome with nerves she fainted and the following year Angela Clarke's knickers slowly descended in the middle of her monologue. So you could say that this year's episode was not unexpected.

I will never ever forgot my first Sunday School encounter with Judith, at the tender age of three. 'Oh Margaret, do come and meet Judith. I know you two will get on so well together!'

Dolly France was trying a little too hard to encourage the two wide-eyed toddlers standing in front of her to join hands and make friends. Her face beamed encouragement but I was having none of it.

Shy and overwhelmed I quickly hid behind my mother's skirts, cautiously peeping out at Judith, who was likewise rooted to the spot. Neither of us had ever met or played with many children of our own age, so we were both understandably fazed by the new experience. Little wonder really, as way back in the forties there were no such things as play groups or mother and toddler circles, except perhaps for a few expensive private kindergartens. Those were the days of food rationing, the building of post-war pre-fabs for the homeless, gardens with air raid shelters instead of grass and the inception of the NHS.

Dolly France took us both gently by the arm and sat us down side by side on an uncomfortable bench in the tiny chapel vestibule. There was only one opaque glass window high up, plaster was peeling off the ceiling and the room smelled of red floor polish. The walls were bare apart from a few posters out of Child Education magazine, showing animals on a farm and a family attending church.

'This is the Nursery Department. You're going to have such fun. We learn nursery rhymes and sing songs, then there are puzzles and the art corner where you can paint lovely pictures of Jesus.' She was in full flood now, totally ignoring the scared faces gazing up at her.

I wasn't sure who Jesus was but hoped he would be a nice, kind man like Father Christmas. I dared to glance at my new companion, admiring her beautifully curled ringlets, tied up with a red satin bow and her pleated tartan kilt and Clark's brown t-bar sandals, probably purchased from Lawson and Stockdale like my own. Despite my nerves I thought that Judith looked nice and that we might become friends.

She must have been having similar thoughts, as she reached out her hand and said. 'Hello Margaret.'

I was too tongue-tied to reply but managed to nod and flash her a special smile, something I knew appealed to strangers. When I was out in town shopping with my mother, acquaintances would sometimes stop to chat and at my mother's bidding I would smile and politely say hello. They always commented on my charming smile.

So began a deep friendship, an inseparable bond, which was to last a lifetime. We were like sisters. When Judith sadly died of cancer some fifty years later, I stood at her grave, tears steaming down my cheeks, remembering that scene in the Nursery room like it was only yesterday. Closing my eyes to block out the cold graveyard under hard frost and the tearful mourners with their floral tributes, I murmured under my breath, 'Dear Judith, how lucky were we? Our friendship was indestructible. Death will never part us.'

Like our parents before us, Judith and I were expected to attend chapel regularly. North East Lincolnshire was a stronghold of Methodism, the place where its founder, John Wesley, had lived. Sunday afternoons meant Sunday School, which we both generally enjoyed. Of course we soon became familiar with this mysterious Jesus person. At story time we would gather round our young teacher in a circle and hear a story from the Bible, in which Jesus usually played a prominent role. This was generally followed by an art session, a chance to depict the story we had heard using coloured crayons. Once the pianist started playing a gentle tune, everyone knew it was time to clear away and move their chairs back into neat rows.

I loved the Primary Class, especially as my Aunt Jessie was in charge there, so I felt very at ease. Aunt Jessie was also a primary school teacher and liked to stretch the youngsters by testing their knowledge. I recall some of her questions which elicited honest but extremely amusing answers. A particularly memorable one was about the people who roamed the desert sands.

'Does anyone know the name of those people?' Aunt Jessie asked.

Most of the children shook their heads but one eager little lad on the front row was bursting to give the answer. He announced triumphantly, 'Please, miss, I know, I know … It's the Roaming Catholics.'

The next stage up was Juniors, a much bigger section,

and then when you were really grown up and cool you moved up to the Seniors. This class was held in a horribly smelly room, narrow and depressing. It was called 'the gas chamber' or sometimes the 'gaslight chamber'. Absolutely nothing whatsoever to do with Hitler or the horror of the concentration camps; it was simply lit by gas lights and as you may well imagine the resulting smell made it a rather undesirable place to be!

*The old frontage of Mill Road Methodist Church
as I knew it in childhood*

The 'Gas(light) Chamber'

Mill Road Methodist church,
my family almost lived there!
Sundays saw us there in our best clothes, twice!

A barn of a building, full of
high-ceilinged rooms and vestibules.
No central heating then and no
electric lights in one wing.
Senior bible class was forced
to meet in a long, thin room,
dismal in the extreme, ensuring
no teenager dwelt on ungodly thoughts!
Lit by a central gas light, emitting
an evil smell like rotten eggs,
affectionately known as the 'Gas(light) Chamber'.

Our teacher was old Tom Elsey,
his brain addled with dementia,
(although no one mentioned that).
The scriptures tripped off his tongue
in a torrent of confusion – bible stories
all back to front, muddled names.

Some of the teenage boys came
just for a laugh, tormented him,
singing obscenities in the guise of hymns

Long since demolished, the chapel's name
has changed; St Andrew's now,
rebuilt in contemporary style,
a temple of stainless steel and glass.
But to me it will always be Mill Road.
Even today former pupils still reminisce
about Sunday School in the 'Gas(light) Chamber'.

With Auntie Jessie, aged 6

Gladys, our Austin 7, with my dad inside

Sunday Afternoons
on the Wolds

We named her Gladys, painted her maroon and black,
commanded her to take us to the land of make-believe

She willingly climbed the wolds, coughing and sputtering,
hope cranking the reluctant engine, a bird in stiff-winged flight

We free-wheeled down the bosoms of lush pastures,
passing newborn lambs suckling their mother's milky wisdom

Furrows newly ploughed after garnering of the grain
morphed seamlessly into bleak midwinter wastelands,

gingerbread houses with white iced roofs,
eagerly awaiting the visit of Saint Nicholas

Bright-eyed and eager we jumped out of the car,
stepping through the looking glass into a wonderland,

catching the feathered weave of air-borne magic
threading through seven oak wood and down to heron brook,

souls dreaming of flaming dragons and knights on horseback,
secret quests hidden from everyone but ourselves

We gathered leaves from dewy pools in mossy hollows;
time an irrelevance in this place of breathtaking mystery

The silk smock of spring slipped seamlessly into summer garb,
childhood was released to guilt-free games in the sun —

Yet bitter-sweet on the tongue a different
   confection lingered …
an unknown rite of passage into responsible
   adulthood

Celebrating Harvest Festival

As a child my favourite time of year, apart from Christmas, was Harvest Festival. There were huge celebrations at school and in chapel. What I loved most of all was driving over the Lincolnshire Wolds with my parents in Gladys, our old Austin 7, in late September/ early October and seeing the rich deep brown of the ploughed fields rolling away into the distance. I loved the stark contrast of the brown fields, green grass, yellow corn stooks and colourful trees with their myriad tumbling leaves; coppers, golds and russet reds, forming an autumnal backdrop.

The Lincolnshire Wolds are a well-kept secret; an area of incredible beauty, especially in autumn, away from the usual tourist track. Those who chance upon the area return frequently to its peaceful beauty. The following poem celebrates fond memories of childhood harvests, bringing a warm, cosy glow to my cheeks.

Autumn Blows In

The Spirit of Autumn paints the local canvas dusky red
With splashes of gold and green within a vibrant labyrinth.
Departing birds hold court in rows, high up on the ancient plinth
Around the old village cross where trysting lovers used to wed.
Ploughed fields are bare, the harvest home has safely been brought in again
Nights start to lengthen, soon the hours of indolence begin to wane.

Nature's glorious hoard is piled up high in the local chapel;
A stunning show of pumpkins, marrows, peppers and courgettes,
Trugs of tomatoes, ripened fruit, large red onions in their nets,

Arranged along the altar rail a row of gleaming apples.
The heady, languid days of Summer heat have sadly long-since fled
Mischievous Autumn takes his brush and paints earth's dying canvas red.

My parents and me, in Grandma and Granddad Browning's back garden

Walking with my mum, aged 4

My imaginary friends

As a young child I was labelled 'highly strung' and people commented that I had a vivid imagination. Those who are only-children like myself have no siblings to play with or bounce their ideas off, so they often create their own imaginary world. Mine was filled with unusual characters drawn from the urban landscape around me. My dolls and soft toys became real people.

One of my favourites was a large, pink pig, dressed like a doll in a blue gingham frock with blue shoes on its trotters. I called her Mrs Pig and really adored her. Her close companion was a character by the surprising name of Mrs Geyser! This originated from the allotments which backed onto the eightfoot at the side of our bungalow – a broad passageway via which you accessed our back door and the repair garage and sheds behind the garden.

These allotments were mostly neglected but some were used for growing fruit and vegetables and one of them boasted a tall greenhouse. It was opposite my bedroom window and had a short, metal chimney sticking through the roof which emitted a spiral of grey smoke from time to time. My mum told me it was a geyser, a concept which of course I didn't understand at that tender age. For me it represented a magical kind of person and so I created the fictitious character Mrs Geyser.

Whenever my mum took me shopping with her it was of great importance that Mrs Pig and Mrs Geyser came too. I would merrily chat to them as we walked along, telling them stories and reciting nursery rhymes. My mum just smiled and never discouraged me from this in any way. I realise it must have looked odd to passersby, especially when I stopped at lampposts and pretended to unlock the small door in the base and speak to an imaginary creature living in there. I saw these as being tiny doors to fairy dwellings and thought it rude to pass them by without saying hello to the inhabitants.

I remember clearly how on one occasion I was bending down pretending to unlock the fairy door with my special key, chatting all the while to Mrs Pig and Mrs Geyser when a woman strolled by and paused to watch my activities.

She shook her head in disbelief and with a sad look on her face turned to my mother and said, 'Oh dear me, what a shame, such a pretty little thing to be suffering mental illness like that.'

I can't now recall if my mother replied or tried to explain the situation, but I do recall the look of pity on the woman's face, which I didn't understand at all!

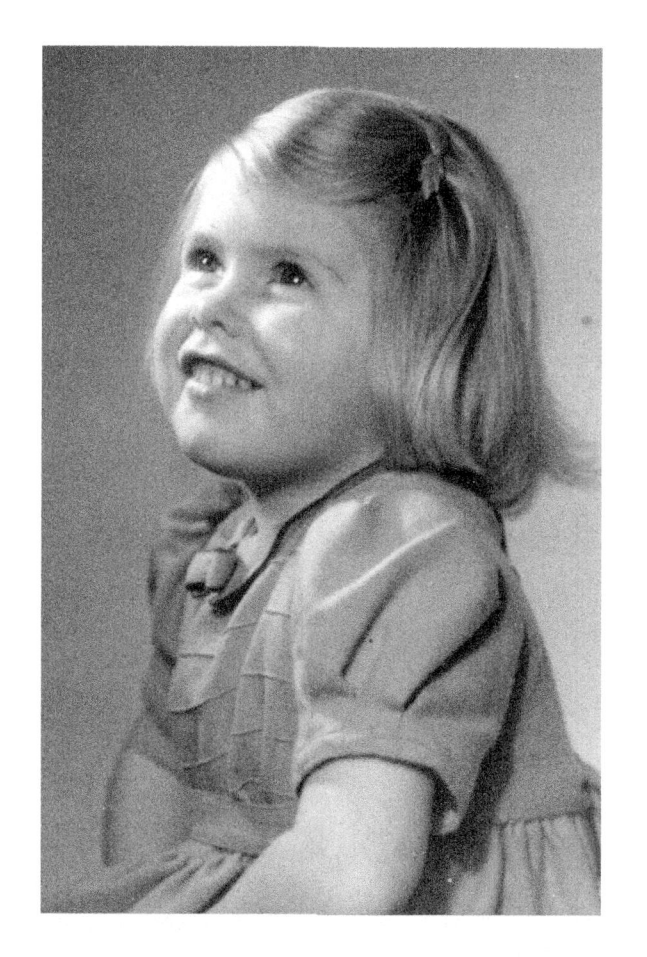

Aged 3

With Grandma and Granddad Browning, aged 3

Grandma and Granddad Browning

Queen of all she surveyed,
barking orders from her capacious armchair,
pride prohibiting use of an ear-trumpet.

Her ample bosoms heaving beneath lace shawls,
her fox-fur draped over the velvet chaise,
its spiteful jaws always snarling.

Inching her arthritic frame forwards,
she would reach for the curling tongs on the coals,
her thickened ankles poking out

from beneath voluminous black skirts
Bones so lithe and supple in youth
wistfully remembering past frivolities.

She would startle at the rag-and-bone-man's cries,
her husband, stooped from years of hard graft,
shuffled off, spade in hand, to collect fresh manure

Her grey hair sizzled between the tongs,
neat rows of Jean Harlow waves
struggling to flatter her ageing features

Fifty years together, golden memories
sandwiched between layers of stark reality,
love tokens mistakenly exchanged for monotony

Darby and Joan, living out their twilight years
in humble surroundings … a god-fearing couple
each in an enclave inaccessible to the other

Lady with Lavender Aura

From a secret drawer Aunt Jessie
takes the unctuous lavender oil ... and

gaggles of barefoot children run amok through
wildflower meadows, dry tongues of summer

yearning for sarsaparilla and calamine balm
to soothe the itch of post-war deprivation.

She hears the electric hum of bees in lupin throats,
watches fingers pluck flowers from air-raid shelter walls,

Breathes in carbolic soap from the hard-scrubbed nails
of her dad, stripped off to wash in the kitchen sink,

Drools as her mum lifts milk-topped scones from
the blackened side-oven – Mrs Beaton's, of course

On elbow crooks and freckled wrists she drips
the oil, cuts on her fingers stinging like vinegar

Too much! intoxicating, filling her school-teacher head
with sickly-sweet confusion – gasping for breath,

wheezing from the burn of excess, as though
the lavender fields might soon be pulped to dust –

Those fields in France, crackling with spit-roast
hedgehogs, where carefree gypsies danced, caroused

and jumped the devil's cinders, their nostrils teased
by a lavender sea, fused with basil and thyme,

An idyll in a bottle, nostalgia released each time
Aunt Jessie performed her daily toilette,

Her clockwork days marked out in rhythmic bursts,
Obedient daughter, cherished by her family

*Auntie Jessie May Browning as bridesmaid to
my mum and dad*

Nanny Kate Buttle in the front garden at Sherburn Street

Nanny Buttle's Pork Chops

Glossary:
Eightfoot – a rough passageway between buildings (about 8 feet wide)
Looking rare and black ower bull's mother's noo – it's grey and dark, bad weather is coming
Siling – pouring with rain
Skelled – tipped (over)
Snecking – being nosy

Nanny Buttle sang as she worked,
a Methodist hymn learnt in chapel
Her 'country ways' annoyed my dad
He raised his eyebrows when she
slurped her cooled down tea
from a saucer, *so common!*
or covered the quarry-tiled floor
with newspaper in bad weather
'It's siling down, mind yersen' she would scold.

Wednesday being laundry day
she came to help my mum –

a complicated task
requiring zinc copper, dolly posher
scrubbing board and mangle,
all stowed safely away in the 'glory hole'
Hairnet gripped securely in place,
gingham overall with sleeves rolled up
she stood ready for another hard day's graft.

Corky the cat always knew she was coming,
slinking off, crouching on the brick wall
at the bottom of the eightfoot patiently waiting,
aware Wednesdays meant Nanny's pork chops.
If he was patient and resisted the urge
to dash between busy legs, he might get the scraps.
Nanny was not a cat-lover, often chiding him
'Stop yer snecking! Yer by near skelled it!'

A country lass at heart, Nanny always relied on
phases of the moon in Old Moore's Almanac.
Thunderstorms panicked her, so she
kept a close eye on gathering black clouds
'Looking rare and black ower bull's mother's noo'
she observed, and with the first clap of thunder
she was off like a greyhound to hide under the stairs.
Quick as a flash Corky would steal her pork chop!
Mission accomplished for him.

Great Aunts Jessie
and Nellie

Historical note:
Great Aunts Jessie and Nellie were Granddad Browning's sisters. Queen Street Place Cottages, where they lived, were demolished and the site redeveloped to meet modern requirements.

The image is still so clear:
a simple two-up-two-down,
crudely furnished, smothered in dust,
its cardboard characters spun from lives
of drudgery in the local factories,
stooped bodies witness to spartan living

Great Aunt Nellie swathed in shawls
squatting on her three-legged stool;
her sister Jessie, dripping pail in hand,
returning from her trek to the spring
a life stripped bare to the bones;
cooking simple meals over the fire,
repairing laddered stockings by gaslight.

The piano in the parlour groaned
beneath nests of wooden dolls, tubs of spills,
whittled by idle hands in slack times …
On Sundays hymns were belted out full throttle,
eyes shining in the flicker of candlelight.

Out in the yard a crude wooden privy yawned,
Old Aunt Sara's sacking coat, limp on its
peg, offering comfort to generations
of reluctant visitors in inclement weather.

For this wide-eyed slip of a girl,
escaping strict parental ties, it offered
a chance to be Alice-in-Wonderland …
Sadly this little gem was demolished decades ago
Victorian propriety replaced by modern convenience.

Great aunts Jessie and Nellie on Cleethorpes Prom

Me and Granddad Browning at Hubbards Hills, Louth

Visits to Louth and the nearby Hubbards Hills

Louth lies at the foot of the Lincolnshire Wolds where they meet the Lincolnshire Marsh, having developed where the ancient trackway along the Wolds, known as the Barton Street, crosses the River Lud.

The town is situated to the east of a gorge carved into the Wolds that forms the Hubbard's Hills, a natural park. As a child I often visited with my mum, my aunt Jessie and the great aunts. It was quite a journey to get there, although in reality Louth is only 16 miles from Cleethorpes and with modern cars and roads takes only 20-30 minutes.

We would take the No.6 bus from Cleethorpes to Grimsby and then take the Louth bus, which meandered through all the rural villages, stopping at every pillar and gatepost, as my dad would say, pausing for a break halfway at Holton-le-Clay. The journey took a good hour. Once there we would have lunch with the great aunts in their quaint cottage then walk to Hubbards Hills and spend the afternoon wandering through the valley by the shallow river, me hopping across stepping stones, scrambling up the steep valley sides and buying an ice-cream in the café.

This was a magical excursion for me, a chance to escape to a place which held me in its thrall. Nowadays it has, of course, been commercially developed but to this day Louth has retained many beautiful and quirky period properties and is often described as 'a place time forgot', giving visitors the distinct feeling that they have stepped back in time.

One of its other attractions is St James' Church with its remarkably tall spire, which visitors can climb. Louth also still has a cattle market, the last in Lincolnshire. Many of the independent shops have retained frontages from a bygone age, but of course the town was never built to carry heavy traffic through its narrow streets. There is now a one-way system in place and car parking can be difficult, most of the car parks being quite compact. When we visited in 2019 through-traffic was heavy and car parking not so easy in the centre.

I noted, however, that on the whole Louth has been able to retain its *olde worlde* charm. The pace of life here is most certainly less hurried and stressful. If you ever get the chance to stop there and take a stroll around for a few hours you will not be disappointed.

Bursar County Primary Junior School, Cleethorpes

Starting infants' school was the first major trauma in my life, still so clear in my mind. I had never socialised with other children, apart from once a week at Sunday School, so the shock of being wrenched from my mother and put in a prefabricated classroom with thirty or more other youngsters was a nightmare. I howled loudly and inconsolably.

The class teacher, Miss Nottle, eventually sat me on her knee and stroked my hair in an effort to calm me down. Luckily my maternal grandmother, Nanny Buttle, lived almost opposite the school gates, so at lunchtime I could be collected by my mum and taken over there.

Lunch hours were longer than they are nowadays. School started at 9am and the morning session finished at 12 noon. Afternoon school recommenced at 1:30pm, so there was a break of one and a half hours. This meant that, when older, I could walk home to Sherburn Street to have lunch and had plenty of time to relax and return for the afternoon session, which finished at 4pm.

Sherburn Street was a good mile away from Bursar Street, which meant I walked four miles to and from school every day. No wonder post-war children were skinny and healthy! Our diet was also much more restricted and I recall that we had ration books and had to exchange the coupons for goods. Sweets were rationed and I clearly remember my family having one Mars bar per week. My dad would cut it into slices and we would enjoy one slice each. Little wonder that many children today suffer from obesity!

We usually had a cooked, healthy lunch with plenty of vegetables on the plate. At teatime we had something simple like beans on toast, cheese on toast, a boiled egg, cod's roe with vinegar sprinkled over or bread and dripping. For me a great favourite was Marmite (as it still is today). Marmite thinly spread on pikelets (thin crumpets) was a real treat.

As my mum was a talented baker, there was always an array of cakes on offer: fairy cakes, butterfly cakes, rock buns, melting moments, almond slices, maids of honour or a mouth-watering chocolate sponge cake, all beautifully set out on a posh two-tier cake stand, complete with doilies.

Class sizes at primary school were large compared with today. Pupils were placed in four streams, A B C D – A being the top one. In my last two years at junior school there were forty-four pupils in my class! Discipline had to be rigid and of course corporal punishment was the norm. Bad behaviour meant you were given the cane, the slipper, smacked across the legs or cuffed around the ear.

For fear of painful punishment and humiliation pupils were kept in line. Nobody dared to speak, titter, poke an annoying neighbour in the ribs or pass notes in class. If discovered doing so, the consequences would be dire.

Some teachers, however, were sadistic and picked on certain children, including those less fortunate or less intelligent. They were sometimes singled out for what I can only describe as brutal beatings, which scared the rest of the class half to death. I recall boys being made to stand in the corner with a dunce's hat on for a whole session!

Aged 5

The Episode with the Psalm and the Bishop

The Headmaster strode smiling into class –
We rose, slightly concerned,
imagining we might be in trouble

'Would Margaret Browning please stand up?'
Why was I being singled out?
I nervously went to stand by his side.

'Margaret, your psalm has brought great joy
to our bishop, in his illness,
Maurice Lincoln has sent you a thank you gift.'

I gasped. This was totally unexpected.
A bishop, a gift, how come?
I fidgeted nervously in disbelief.

By way of explanation,
poetry was my thing,
I loved to write poems and psalms,

influenced by our Methodist chapel,
by Sunday school and my lay-preacher father
my scribblings had a religious slant

My classmates applauded loudly
as I opened the cardboard box …
Would it be chocolates? I really hoped so!

To my great dismay no chocolates!
In the box was the book of common prayer
with a letter of blessing from the bishop.

My heart sank. What good was that?
We weren't even C of E! We Methodists
had our own hymn books.

With hindsight of course I understood
the honour bestowed on me. I still have
the book and letter; cherished possessions now.

More About My Parents

My mother didn't have a job while I was at school. She was a housewife, as many mothers were in those days. My father had his own gentleman's outfitters shop in the main street in Cleethorpes town centre, St Peter's Avenue. Unfortunately he hit a bad patch trade-wise and had to give it up. For a time he was out of work but eventually became a sales representative (travelling salesman as they were called then) for a large company, GUS (Great Universal stores).

He had a large territory to cover and had a succession of increasingly large cars to use, beginning with a pale blue car which we named Rylma and ending up with an Austin Maxi estate in racing green. The cases of samples he had to drag around with him were extremely heavy and as he aged the job really became too much for him. I realise how greatly he must have suffered heaving the samples in and out of shops.

My parents were anxious for me to take up every opportunity possible and happily paid out for piano lessons, singing lessons, elocution lessons and ballet classes (not all at the same time, I hasten to add). With hindsight, I was always busy attending one thing or another and felt obliged to become as proficient as possible at each one. Along the way I entered many competitions and won medals and trophies for dance and solo singing. To be truthful, however, I did find this sometimes too arduous, mainly because I was always so nervous and stressed pre-performance and I felt that too much pressure was being put on me.

Cadets sing Margaret's own hymn

A two-verse hymn, the words for which were written by a nine-years-old Girls' Life Brigade cadet, Margaret Browning, of Sherburn-street, Cleethorpes, was sung by cadets of the 1st Cleethorpes Company of the Girls' Life Brigade at the company's annual harvest thanksgiving and presentation of awards at Mill - road Methodist Church, Cleethorpes.

Margaret, who was eight when she wrote the hymn, was introduced to the congregation of parents by the minister, the Rev. H. Gregory Taylor.

Later she carried off the Cadet Cup. Ann Gladwin won the Junior Cup, and Ann Soulsby gained the Senior trophy.

The commandant of the Grimsby and District Battalion of the G.L.B., Capt. Mrs. V. M. Cook, made the presentations, and reports were given by the company captain Miss G. M. Hoult, and the cadet leader, Miss D. France.

The Rev. Gordon Parkhouse, minister of Beaconthorpe Methodist Church, Cleethorpes, gave an address, and Audrey Winfarrah conducted the service.

Receiving the Cadet Cup after writing a hymn

Washday Wednesdays

On windy washdays Mum was stressed.
Wind chimes clanked and jangled
in the fierce gale. Washing flapped wildly

on the clothes line – a string of ghostly bodies
on the hangman's gallows,
bloated corpses with distorted limbs.

In the lull between gusts you might catch
the crackle of sweet wrappers in forgotten pockets,
loose buttons tapping out morse-code messages.

Across the lawn crumpled leaves,
as lined as Nanny Buttle's street-map face,
went chasing ceaselessly back and forth.

The tight-lipped dolly pegs swung
like pendulums with each new assault.
Yet their resistance proved too much

for the wind's frenzied onslaught.
He would turn on the sulking clouds
with their churlish attitude …

Something had to give,
Someone had to bend to his will
before he blew himself out.

With a frown on her face, hair tied up in a turban,
my mum pushed the damp clothes through the mangle
Wilfred Pickles would often be chatting on the radio

I knew it was best to make myself scarce
So I often crept off to my bedroom with a book,
knowing I could read my Enid Blyton tales undisturbed.

Fish and Chips

Glossary:
Scraps – tiny slivers of batter detached from fish in frying process, heaped on top of chips

You've not eaten fish and chips
unless you've been to Steele's
in Cleethorpes market place

or queued at one of the many
chippies on street corners –
one at the end of every road

You would see the signs
'Frying Tonight' and that meant
with beef dripping – a world of difference!

The menu was comprehensive:
haddock, cod, skate, rock salmon
and of course 'scraps' were free

though positively unhealthy!
But we didn't know or care back then –
they 'piled 'em high' and we drooled!

Tea in Guy and Smith's Cafe

Glossary:
On appro – short for on approval

Saturday afternoons were special;
we caught the number six to Grimsby,
famed for its docks and fishing,
yet often the butt of comedians' jokes

Uptown there were higher-end shops,
their goods more upmarket, plus a department store –
Guy and Smith's – you knew you'd arrived
when you had tea in the elegant café there.

The waiting staff were dressed like
Downton Abbey clones – black dresses,
white aprons and frilled white caps,
deferentially taking the order,

bringing you china cups and elegant
teapots – starched white napkins 'de rigueur'
We ordered Welsh rarebit or poached
eggs on toast, in summer: banana splits.

My mum would take her laddered nylons
to the Bull Ring haberdashers for repair.
I sometimes took a doll to the dolls' hospital …
Make do and mend was the norm – not so nowadays!

If Guy and Smith's was uptown, then downtown
was Freeman Street shopping centre, where we bought
school uniform from Lawson and Stockdale's –
my clothes taken 'on appro' for my dad's opinion.

We might then catch the trolley bus home,
alight at the Lifebuoy Pub near the seafront,
giggle at drunken sailors fighting the revolving doors …
The simple things in life were pleasure enough back then!

To London by Steam Train

In my childhood there was a railway line direct from Cleethorpes to London, the East Lincolnshire Line which used to operate under steam. It was opened in 1848 and closed finally in 1970.

I was always very excited to travel down to the 'big smoke' as it was nicknamed on a steam train. The thrill of hearing that chuff chuff as the train pulled out of the station and increased its speed, then the clickety clack, clickety clack as the wheels sped along. The coaches were sub-divided into compartments for about 8 people which we entered via a long corridor. There were upholstered bench seats on either side facing each other and luggage nets overhead.

The route passed through sleepy market towns such as Louth, Alford, Burgh-le-Marsh, to larger places like Boston, Peterborough and then finally to King's Cross Station in London. There were porters on the larger station platforms, always ready to assist with your luggage (as long as you tipped them suitably) but no barriers to enter or exit station platforms.

When we alighted at our destination my mother insisted we went to thank the train driver for getting us there safely.

How sweet was that? The younger generation hoot with laughter when I tell them that. I recall how the engine driver would often be descending from his cab as we walked past and always had time for a quick chat. Those were the days of relaxed travel, sadly now consigned to history. How different things were!

With a friend in the back garden of Sherburn Street, aged 8

My first year at Grammar School

The Clementina Clee Years: Life at Grammar School

At the age of eleven, I won a coveted place at Cleethorpes Grammar School for Girls by passing the dreaded 11+ exam and I became a 'Clementina Clee'. This exam instilled fear into every pupil. If you passed you went to the local grammar school. If you failed you went to a secondary modern school or perhaps to a technical school if it was thought you might go into a trade or other vocation.

The ensuing seven years at Cleethorpes Girls' Grammar School were a magical period in my life. I was in my element, as I started learning foreign languages plus Latin, to which I had always been attracted. That was where my strengths lay.

School Speech Day was a big annual event held on Cleethorpes Pier. It was a grand occasion to showcase pupils' achievements. Subject prizes were awarded and I am proud to have received the modern languages prize several times. The whole school lustily sang the school song *Non Nobis, Domine – not unto us o Lord* and there was always a distinguished guest speaker, usually rather boring but our impeccable Clementina manners made us sit in quiet reverence, twiddling our fingers.

The school anthem sent shivers down my spine, especially

when we built towards the climax with ever-increasing volume until the final, high notes of *Non Nobis Do-o-o-mi…ne!* Thunderous applause usually followed at which our headmistress, known affectionately as 'the Dev' turned and beamed at her audience and I tried to find my proud parents in the crowd to flash them a quick smile.

During these years I was given the opportunity to learn the cello, sing in the choir and join the Grimsby, Cleethorpes and District Youth Orchestra. Each of these provided me with skills and experiences which broadened my horizons. In the upper sixth, I did a German exchange with a penfriend in Kaiserslautern and sampled for the first time a culture very different from my own. I have written a separate chapter about this German adventure, as it made a huge impression on me.

For the most part I am still in touch with the grammar school girlfriends in my form, Jackie, Angela and Marie. Our connection is as strong as ever. We have all somehow managed to finish up living within a 50 mile radius of Cleethorpes and meet up regularly to catch up. We still fondly reminisce about amusing episodes, our teachers and fellow pupils, how we dressed for PE, silly things we said, rebellious classmates and so forth. Such friendships are a joy and last forever.

I am so grateful for the education I received, which later allowed me to study at university and opened many doors in life for me – a girl from a humble, god-fearing lower middle class background. After my A levels, I went up to Durham to study Honours German with French. I was the first in my family to go to university and in those days it was an opportunity taken up by only a small percentage of school leavers. I was lucky enough to be awarded a Lindsey Senior Scholarship, which covered a large proportion of the costs, but I believe my parents, who were not well-off, must have made huge sacrifices to keep me there and support me financially. I owe them a huge debt of gratitude.

Receiving an award from Miss D. E. Vallins,
Headmistress of Cleethorpes Girls' Grammar School

Clementina Clees

Clementina Clees – this was the headmistress' affectionate nickname for the pupils at Cleethorpes Girls Grammar School. They nicknamed their headmistress 'The Dev'

This poem is dedicated to my fellow Clementinas; Jackie, Angela, Marie and Judith

With age our birthplace lures us back,
our instinct turns again to the once familiar
buildings we frequented day to day,
people we knew and loved so dearly;
They nurture us, like a child's comforter,
a sheltered haven in a stormy sea

I am fortunate that I still boast
loyal friends from childhood days;
ex Clementina Clees from school,
always under the Dev's watchful eye:
Dorothy Elizabeth Vallins,
our illustrious headmistress, strong moral
compass throughout our grammar school years

That unspoken code is still in place,
the sisterhood survives the stormy seas.
We know precisely where we stand in life
(More recent friendships lack intrinsic depth).

With time I've come to appreciate
our birthright is a special gift …
Nothing endures the test of time
like friendships rooted in the past,
nurtured in that place we first called home.

M J B

It seemed a kindness,
not a thoughtless act
that caused my mother's frown.
Just a fountain pen,
my initials engraved on the side,
lent to a friend in class
when hers stopped working

My mother's expectations
were sometimes pitched too high.
Nine out of ten was good, praised,
but of course ten would be even better!
I studied the initials, M J B,
failing at first to grasp
another meaning beyond their link to me …
An 'M' for moderation – my mother,
between failure and perfection
no shades of grey for her;
for me a half-way compromise was good,
could I not fail just a little?

Then 'J' for Jessie, my aunt,
the embodiment of patience;
her quiet smile afforded me
the possibility of being
purely and simply ME, warts and all

Finally a 'B', perhaps for books,
my escape to an alternative reality,
a place where my mind was free
to indulge my imagination,
to dream my childhood dream
of becoming a writer.

My Friend Ann

When I moved up to grammar school, many of my friends from primary school were there too, so there were many familiar faces in my form, but there were new faces too from other primary schools in the area. One girl stood out from the rest, having come from a private school. Her name was Ann and I discovered she lived quite close to me, although in a much grander house.

We somehow became better acquainted (though I don't recall how exactly this came about) and remained firm friends for many years. Her parents sent her away to boarding school in Harrogate after our first year at grammar school but we still met up in the holidays. Her life was quite different from mine, but somehow we gelled. Maybe it was a case of opposites attract?

My First Taste of Privilege

Two worlds collided seamlessly, for childhood innocence knows no boundaries apart from those that are self-imposed or skewed by adult perceptions

An Unusual Friendship

She had a confident air,
a certain *je ne sais quoi,* which
set her apart from the rest of us

We were in awe of this girl, with her
delicate skin and milk-white pallor –
speaking with received pronunciation,

no local accent or dialect phrases
distinguishable … She came from another world,
unfamiliar to us. I was intrigued.

Others were quick to label her posh,
a breed apart, but I, curious,
empathetic beyond my tender years

sought to explore this otherness,
step out beyond my comfort zone.
A curious friendship blossomed between us

Her Family Home

Her family owned a fine mansion,
set in an elegant part of town where
money talked and bought lavish lifestyles

It stood in landscaped gardens, complete
with orchard, allotment and gardener.
Indoors a billiard room and ballroom stunned

with parquet floor and Louis X1Vth mirrors.
Even back in the 1950s the kitchen
boasted both dishwasher and freezer

We had neither fridge, TV nor washing machine
yet for her this was normality,
for me it was the epitome of cool –

I keenly felt this should be my birthright too …
that Fate had somehow dealt me a lesser hand –
leaving me on the outside – a stranger looking in

Rent Collection in the Rolls Royce

Her grandpa was a well known public figure,
Property owner, businesses of choice
On Saturdays we sometimes drove around
collecting rent with him; from his Rolls Royce
we eagerly smiled out at passers by,
gave them a cheeky wave, as everywhere
the townsfolk deferentially stepped back,
surprised to see the gleaming car parked there.
My family had a modest Austin Seven,
a banger Dad had done up, truth be told
It took us out on sunny weekend jaunts
for picnics by the sea or on the wolds
For me these Rolls Royce outings were a blast –
Pretending that I'd found my niche at last

Girls Life Brigade with Judith in my living room
(I'm on the left and Judith is third from the left)

Awkward Moments in the Royal Albert Hall, London

As young teenagers Judith and I belonged to an organisation for girls at the chapel, similar to the Guides and with broadly similar aims. We were members of the Girls Life Brigade and had to wear itchy navy serge uniforms with berets and white gloves (when on parade).

We both hated parade days, not enjoying being stared at as we marched down St Peter's Avenue two by two to the ear splitting band music of the Boys Brigade. How humiliating it was to see some of my classmates from school giggling at us from the pavement!

There was an upside though. One of the badges we could achieve was for 'International Friendship', which required us to write to children in a country overseas describing our lives in Britain, our families, schools, hobbies and interests by means of a series of letters. To our amazement our team won the UK challenge and were privileged to collect a trophy in a ceremony at the Royal Albert Hall. Oh the excitement! Neither Judith nor I had ever been to London and the thought of the trip was thrilling.

The four girls in our team and our Captain, caught the

steam train from Cleethorpes to King's Cross and stayed the night in a boarding house. I was really worried because I had been told that we would have to travel on the tube to get to the rehearsal the next morning. I had no concept of what this might entail. The only tube I could think of was the glass tube thermometer my mother used to measure my temperature with when I was ill and my brain simply could not translate this into a means of underground transport.

Judith's mother had made things worse by saying it was often crowded and people had to squeeze together so the doors could shut. The picture in my head terrified me and I worked myself up into a panic.

Our Captain laughed when I confessed my fear and put me straight on what to expect. Relieved, I was happy to try it out but couldn't wait to get off at the other end!

The trophy was to be presented to us by Lady Frances Shand Kydd (mother of Princess Diana). Excitement mounted as the day progressed and we lined up in our horrid uniforms to march down the long flight of steps to the arena. All went well on the way down, but on the way back up Judith had another of her clumsy moments, tripping on the stairs and causing the whole line behind to tumble like dominoes. Quick as a flash I hauled her back up and, dignity restored, we exited the arena – but I teased her mercilessly about it for years to come!

As a reward for performing well we were treated to tea and buns in Lyons Corner House but were so exhausted from the excitement of the day that we could hardly keep our eyes open and had to be taxied back to the hotel.

The Girls Life Brigade meetings, though well-intentioned, were sometimes responsible for promoting what today would be labelled 'fake news'. At the tender age of six in the cadet section we had been encouraged to sign the pledge – a practice encouraged by the Methodists in their anti-alcohol campaigns. The initiative had stemmed from a rejection of drunkenness in Victorian times, which led to parents boozing in the alehouses, leaving their young children standing outside, exposed to many dangers. It also often led to increased poverty and domestic abuse.

If you signed the pledge you agreed never to let a sip of alcohol pass your lips in your lifetime! But how damaging it was to indoctrinate young minds and have them sign a document which, at six years old, they were incapable of understanding!

Equally ridiculous was a serious talk the girls were given relating to this. Judith and I laughed our socks off in later years thinking back to what the deputy Captain had said. She forbade us to eat or drink fermented liquids, one of which being vinegar. 'Don't put vinegar on your chips, girls,' she said, 'it's fermented!'

MY TOWN: THEIR LETTERS WIN

FOUR Cleethorpes girls have written letters about their town and district, which together have won joint first place in an "international friendship competition," organised by the Girls' Life Brigade.

With the award goes a cup—and a snag.

For the girls, members of the 1st Cleethorpes Company, Girls' Life Brigade, have tied for first place with a company from Stratford.

One cup . . two teams : . that is the snag.

FOR 6 MONTHS

But everything will be sorted out amicably in London on Sunday when the girls attend a special rally.

There they will be presented with the cup—but only for six months. Stratford will have it for the other six.

The four girls are: Marie Tommon (10), of 98, Highgate; Margaret Browning (11), of 14, Sherburn-street; Judith Smalley (11), of 28, Crowhill-avenue; and Kathleen Smart (11), of 11, Hey-street.

The company commander, Miss G. M. Hoult, points out that the competition was run throughout the British Isles and abroad to help foster international friendship.

About 100 companies entered this year.

The girls were asked to write a letter to an imaginary friend abroad, inviting her for a holiday to this country.

LONDON VISIT

"The letter was expected to contain information about the district the girls lived in, and the amenities and attractions there," Miss Hoult said.

She added that the company was very proud of the four girls and 18 members were travelling to London to see them receive the cup.

"It is a fitting climax to our silver jubilee celebrations," Miss Hoult declared.

MARIE SHOWED THEM THE WAY

A FEW months ago five young Cleethorpes girls sat down to write letters to imaginary pen friends abroad, to explain their life in this country.

It was part of an International Friendship Competition.

The four top scoring girls from each company of the Girls Life Brigade which entered, had their marks totalled, and it has now been disclosed that the 1st Cleethorpes GLB Company are joint winners, with the 4th Stratford.

Youngest member of the Cleethorpes team was Marie Tommon, of 98, Highgate, who is only 10, but was top scorer in her team, with a total of 80 per cent.

Her three team-mates, all of whom are 11, were Margaret Browning, 14, Sherburn Street, Judith Smalley, 28, Crowhill Avenue, and Kathleen Smart, of 11, Hey Street.

The Cleethorpes team must have been one of the youngest in the competition, which was open to G.L.B. companies in the British Isles and overseas.

On Saturday a party from the 1st Cleethorpes travelled to London to see the trophy presented at the G.L.B. Rally at the Albert Hall.

Time off with friends, aged 15: sitting on the canteen wall at Alford with Gillian Wray, Jackie Bullock, Marie Gladwin, Hilary Ford, and me

The Ferry Across the Humber

When we were in our late teens my school friends and I sometimes made a day excursion to the city of Hull, which sits on the bank of the River Humber, opposite the small town of Barton-on-Humber.

In those days the only means of getting to Hull was to take the train from Cleethorpes to New Holland, from where we boarded a paddle-steamer ferry across to Hull. Paddle-steamers were used because they were able to cope with the shallow, shifting sands of the Humber. The river is tidal and on several occasions when crossing at low tide the ferry became stuck on a sandbank. The crew would fetch long, sturdy poles and push them into the sand to try and dislodge the boat.

On one occasion this did not work and we had to wait until the tide turned and the rising water floated us off the bank. The two ferries we most encountered were the *Wingfield Castle* and the *Tattershall Castle*.

The train journey to the ferry terminal took us at a leisurely pace, stopping at country stations and halts, where we would wave to the man in the signal box and the guard in his uniform with his flag and whistle. In spring we would see lambs and calves playing rough and tumble in the fields alongside the track with their siblings or feeding from their mothers, while in autumn we were delighted by the activities of the harvest: enormous combine harvesters droning up and down, golden sheaths of corn stacked in bales (referred to as corn stooks back then) and seagulls following the machinery, keen to dine on the pickings.

Lincolnshire has always been an agricultural county and the everyday activities of farm hands, casual labourers and horse riders would be there on display for us to chat about en route. It was our Lincolnshire, a peaceful backwater that time forgot. I miss those days.

Our destination, Kingston-upon-Hull, usually known simply as Hull, was a city with a greater population than Grimsby. Inland from the thriving fishing docks there were large department stores, art galleries and much to occupy us. It was definitely the place to be. On arrival, we rushed to eat in one of the famous fish and chip restaurants in the city centre. As in Grimsby and Cleethorpes, the best fish and chips could be eaten in Hull, cooked in beef dripping, which makes all the difference.

We loved the opportunity to sample the latest lipstick shades in the cosmetic department, perching on high stools to apply the trendy colours like TNT, a pale, chalky and rather unforgiving shade that was supposed to give you a Marilyn Monroe pout. Our parents would have screamed 'Take it off!' but they were not there and we had the freedom to walk around Hull looking like ghastly clowns if we wanted to. It was a rite of passage, I guess.

We were generally exhausted by mid afternoon so indulged

in a frothy coffee in the nearest Wimpy Bar. Then it was back to the ferry terminal and the journey home, tired but still excited.

Historical note:
The railway company had built a pier at New Holland some 1,500 feet (460 m) in length with the railway station, allowing direct connection with the ferry service. New Holland Pier railway station opened on 1 March 1848 and service ceased in June 1984 when the newly built Humber Bridge was opened,

On Board a Grimsby Trawler

Talking of trains and boats I was reminded of another kind of vessel which had great significance for the local area economy in my youth – the fishing trawler.

Grimsby docks used to be jam-packed with these and the sale of fish was a major contributor to the once-vibrant economy of the region, now sadly in decline since the Cod Wars. The dock tower loomed above the town and by the mid 20th century it was a proud symbol of Grimsby's status as the largest fishing docks in the world. Many wealthy fish merchants lived along the beach front at Cleethorpes in what was deemed a well-to-do area, not far from where I lived.

I was lucky enough to be given a personal guided tour by my friend Marie's father, Tim Tommon, who was the skipper of a Grimsby trawler. He was away from home for long periods of time, leaving his diminutive wife, Emily, to cope with bringing up three children more or less single-handed (and the two boys were definitely a handful, not to mention Marie's outgoing, stubborn personality).

While on shore leave, her father had time to show us around the huge docks, take us aboard his trawler and explain how everything worked.

This experience remains a vivid memory for me. It was

so exciting, stepping into a world I knew nothing about. I remember being appalled by the cramped living conditions on board and wondering how on earth the crew survived the long weeks at sea with such basic facilities. The scale of the fishing operation was huge and I was fascinated to learn how the fish, once caught and hauled aboard in the giant nets, were kept frozen, ready for sale in the dock warehouses on the ship's return.

It was a cold, bleak day when we visited and I could well imagine the appalling conditions the fishermen must often have faced, freezing cold and constantly navigating storms and bad weather out in the rough seas off Iceland and Norway.

Historical note:
Fishing spawned a host of other industries too, such as frozen food production companies, whose brands were household names (and some still are) – for example Birds Eye (where I worked night shifts as a student), Findus, Eskimo and cold-storage companies. Growing up in the area you could not escape the importance of fishing, it provided thousands of jobs for local workers.

Visiting a coffee bar at the White Horse Hotel in Alford, aged 15, with Jackie Bullock, Hilary Ford, Gillian Wray and Angela Davis

A Summer Week in Alford

Complete with coffee bar, juke box and Lady Chatterley's Lover

From a very early age I had always wanted to be a writer. I loved to keep holiday journals.

Recently, I unearthed one written about the Grimsby, Cleethorpes & District Youth Orchestra's summer school week in Alford, Lincolnshire. It was interesting to revisit my take on things as a sixteen year old. Occasionally we had weekends away with the orchestra, usually staying in a school, camping out on the floor and giving a concert on the final afternoon. In Alford we had a whole week, which gave us free time to go into town and explore. It was the era of coffee bars serving frothy coffee, often boasting a trendy jukebox.

*Rehearsing for a Girls' Brigade church event
(I'm second from the right, with the cello)*

'Johnny, Remember Me'

'Johnny, Remember Me' sung by Johnny Leyton was a No.1 hit single in the UK singles chart in 1961

Coffee bars serving frothy coffee,
all the rage in the fifties and sixties.
The *Hacienda* (fondly known as the Hac),
The Hole in the Wall, the *Salamander*;
Exotic Grimsby haunts where teenagers loved to
 hang out;
it was 'cool' to be seen sipping coffee there.
We dolled ourselves up before daring to set foot
 inside.

In August 1961 we holidayed in Alford
with our youth orchestra … a memorable week!
We stayed in a school, camped out on the floor,
had midnight feasts and compared notes on boys.
When rehearsals were over we 'hit the town' –
not that Alford really had much to hit.

To our nervous delight we found a coffee bar,
complete with jukebox featuring the latest hits
and also attracting a bevy of young men
in the prime of their youth, hormones raging.
My friend took a shine to one named Johnny –
to attract his attention she played a hit record
over and over on the jukebox, determined that
he would notice her flirting and ask her out.
'Johnny, remember me,' that was the song –
though he seemed not to notice her at all.

In the end we turned our attention
to secretly reading the naughty bits of
Lady Chatterley's Lover – D H Lawrence's
Novel, banned as indecent back then but a thrill
to find a second-hand flea-market copy …
We hid in a little-used bus-shelter,
deftly located the well-thumbed pages
worth reading, devoured the juicy bits.
Our first taste of freedom, away from home.

In the back garden at Sherburn Street as a teenager

*In my penfriend's living room in Kaiserslautern,
Germany in 1963, painting Easter eggs*

Tasting a Different Culture

I remember thinking that the the rural scenery in The Rhineland Palatinate of Germany was the most beautiful I had ever come across. Quaint half-timbered houses nestled close to decorated wells, cute little shops, sleepy cottages, traditional taverns and cobbled lanes with horses pulling hay carts.

It was Easter 1963 and I was enjoying my first longer trip abroad to stay with my German pen friend and her family in Kaiserslautern. I had decided that I wanted to study German at university and needed to get the top grade in my A level exams in order to secure the university of my choice.

My parents had been rather concerned about my visiting Germany, (or to be totally correct West Germany, as it was then called, being a divided country at that time with East Germany under the communist thumb and completely cut off from the West). It was less than twenty years since the end of WWII and animosity was still rife in the UK, particularly among communities who had suffered badly during the conflict with loss of loved ones in active service, loss of civilians and destruction of homes and infrastructure. My father had not seen active service abroad, having been declared medically unfit and hauled off the train destined for

France at the last moment. He had served at home in the NAAFI in various locations.

My pen friend's father on the other hand had been called up to fight and had lost a lower limb in the conflict. He had a prosthetic leg from the knee down. I recall so clearly how, on my arrival by train in Mainz at four o'clock in the morning I was shocked by what greeted me. I scanned the platform, trying to identify Linde from a black-and-white photo she had sent me and saw her and her father, Eberhard, pushing through the passengers towards me, smiling and waving. To my surprise he was on crutches and clearly disabled. The first thought that flashed through my mind was that my father could have been responsible for wounding him! Ridiculous, of course, as my dad never fought abroad – but just for a brief second that scenario darted through my head and I have never forgotten it.

My next shock was discovering that Linde and her family lived in an exceedingly small flat on the fifth floor of a huge apartment block. They were a family of five – her mother, Annalene, father and two younger sisters, Vera and Gisela. The three girls shared a bedroom which had three small, single beds, one of which was a *Klappbett,* a bed which pulled out of a wall cupboard at night. In order to make room for me the younger sister, Gisela, was sent to stay with her maternal grandparents in Frankfurt for the duration of the school holidays and I slept in her bed.

Linde's parents mostly slept in the lounge on a settee which converted to a large sofa bed, or when other relatives stayed overnight they slept in the tiny dining room, whose table and benches converted into a small double bed. Such ingenuity! In addition there was a tiny kitchen and equally tiny bathroom with toilet, washbasin and bath – but of course no shower, just a rubber hose which attached to the taps. I don't remember it being a squash in the flat but it was certainly not what I had expected. Our bungalow at home was much more spacious.

Kaiserslautern, famous for its football team, was in the sector of West Germany occupied post-war by the Americans, and the town boasted a large American forces' garrison. My pen friend's father worked for an American newspaper there, called The Stars and Stripes. Her mother was a PE teacher at secondary school (the same school that Linde attended). Having two working parents was the norm, it seemed, whereas my mother never had a job until I went to university.

Other surprises for me were the local dialect and the food. I had been learning German for six years prior to my visit and had learned to speak *Hochdeutsch,* high German, the equivalent of Oxford English at the time.

However, just as in the UK, each region of Germany had its own dialect. If you reflect how difficult it can be for us to sometimes understand a Glaswegian or a Liverpudlian, it was the same there. The high German was spoken more in the north and the southern areas spoke with a pronounced dialect. This meant that Linde's family could perfectly well understand my German but I had great difficult initially understanding what they were saying.

I had to tune in my ear and learn completely new words

and expressions. By the end of my month's stay, however, I had got the hang of it and was starting to chat with greater confidence.

I mention food being a shock too. There was no concept of international cuisine as exists nowadays, so encountering another country's food could be a challenge and even things like yoghurt were unknown. We often had Quark, a sour curd cheese, which I simply couldn't stomach. Then there were huge sausages, *Weißwurst,* filled with coarsely minced animal intestines, disgusting to my palate. Hats off to my pen friend's mum who would notice that I was struggling to tackle various dishes and would dash into the kitchen and make me pancakes instead!

On the plus side I loved the delicious cakes which were served up mid afternoon for *Kaffee und Kuchen.* Germans rose early, school started at 8am and many people took an afternoon nap after lunch – the main meal of the day. On waking from our nap, huge pots of coffee were brewed and everyone sat down at the table to enjoy home made fruit tarts, cheese cake, choux pastry buns filled with cream and many other delights. There was always oodles of whipped cream, *Schlagsahne,* and in one month I gained weight and returned home plumper than I had left!

More disappointing was the fact that to me breakfast and evening meal were more or less the same, consisting of a selection of cold cut meats, *Schnittwurst,* and slices of cheese, *Käse,* accompanied by a bread basket bursting with a selection of different breads: white, seeded, black, called *Pumpernickel* and *Knäckebrot,* crisp bread. At breakfast there would also be a selection of home made jams and honey and at the evening meal there might be various salads and picked gherkins. There was never a dessert at evening meal, which I really missed, since the meal we called tea at home always finished with something sweet.

German table manners were different too. Knives were not to be used to cut into a fried egg, for example, and forks held in your right hand were used to scoop up vegetables. Your left hand had to be placed on the table at all times when not using cutlery, not in your lap. Before starting to eat you had to wish everyone *Guten Appetit,* a good appetite.

There were other unspoken rules at that time, which I will mention here (although many may not be relevant in modern-day Germany). Germans never sat on the floor, and men performed a slight click of the heels and slight bow of the head when greeting a lady. There were strict visiting times to adhere to, mostly after the post lunch nap. The same went for telephoning.

Only tradesmen used the back door, visitors went to the front. If you were invited to lunch or coffee you were expected to take a gift – chocolates, flowers, wine or something representing your home country or region. If you took flowers there were strict rules around that too. It had to be an odd number of stems, never even and they had be unwrapped – something that could present logistical difficulties as to what to do with the wrapping paper!

People you didn't know well had to be addressed as Herr X, Frau X or Herr/Frau Doktor X. Only girls were addressed as Fräulein. Once young adults they had to be dignified with the title Frau, whether married or not. Formal titles were always used to address people, which could sometimes result in a complicated start to a conversation. I recall speaking to my pen friend's headmaster, addressing him correctly as Herr Doktor, Professor Emmerich. I couldn't get my mouth round all of that and finished up mumbling something incomprehensible and probably hilarious, judging by the look on his face!

I was struck by the fact that there were many more saints days to celebrate than here, when everything was shut and people spent time with their families. Major religious festivals were celebrated rather differently too. I was able to experience Easter during my stay, which I found a real delight. Children got very excited by the forthcoming visit of the Easter Bunny or *Osterhase,* who would secretly hide chocolate eggs in gardens and woodland on Easter Sunday morning. Of course Easter egg hunts are now commonplace here but not at that time.

Families would make an Easter tree by bringing sturdy forest twigs indoors and arranging them in a tall vase, on which they would hang prettily decorated eggs. Hard boiled eggs were dyed vibrant colours too and arranged on the table for Easter breakfast, along with huge, scrumptious cakes serving ten or twelve people. There were cute table decorations too representing spring and rebirth with the inclusion of cardboard cut-outs of young animals – lambs, chicks, rabbits etc.

Memories of my month in West Germany still remain

vivid in my mind. I was so lucky to live with my pen friend and her family, observing and learning about everyday life in a different culture and improving my language skills. I feel it is so important for young people to be able to travel widely and broaden their horizons. It fosters understanding and tolerance and should be greatly encouraged. I know that I personally benefitted greatly.

On the rag week float at Durham University in 1964

The Aidan's Maidens Years: Life at Durham University

University was undoubtedly the best time of my life. At the time I went up to St Aidan's College, Durham University in 1963 there were around 2,500 students, which meant it was possible to get to know an awful lot of people. What a social whirl! As well as studying hard there was so much to do, new horizons to conquer, clubs and societies to join, theatrical productions to audition for.

My own children laugh when I tell them we each had a 'moral tutor' with whom we had to 'take tea' now and then. Rules for male visitors were strict and the eagle-eyed porter knew exactly which gentleman had gone into the room of which lady. If he hadn't emerged when the bell was rung at 10pm the porter would be banging on the door. Visiting male friends in one of the religious colleges was even more strict. The young men had to put their mattresses out on the landing while they entertained female guests! How ridiculous by today's standards!

Students could not simply come and go as they pleased either and if you wanted to return home during term time for a special family occasion you had to obtain an 'exeat' from the principal herself, Dame Enid Russell-Smith, a black belt in judo no less.

Some evenings we had formal dinner with the principal and her guests seated on a raised dais at high table. Gowns were worn, as they were for attendance at lectures too. You were not permitted to leave the dining room before the principal and on occasions necessitating this you had to stand at the foot of the table and seek permission by 'bowing out,' waiting patiently until Dame Enid saw fit to nod in your direction.

On Thursday evenings there would be a long queue, as it was *Top of the Pops* on TV at 7:30pm and everyone wanted to watch that. Of course we didn't have personal TVs in our rooms and had to crowd round a relatively small set in the Junior Common Room, pushing and shoving to get a viewing spot.

We were keen to see *The Beatles, Rolling Stones* and the famous pop groups of the 60s, plus of course the dance troupe Pan's People doing raunchy numbers to one of the latest hits (at least raunchy for the 1960s, pretty low-key nowadays!) I desperately wanted to be Dee Dee Wilde or Flick Colby – they were so glamorous.

Each college had one formal dance and one informal dance a year – a source of great excitement as to who to invite and what to wear! Many of us made our own dresses (my mum made mine as I have always been a hopeless needlewoman!). Sixties fashion was a big part of the cool girl's style and Saturdays saw many of us taking the bus to Newcastle to buy the latest trendy outfit to wear at the Dunelm Hop. 'Hops' were what discos were called back then. Everyone wanted to be seen and admired.

During my three years there I made copious friends and many of those friendships still survive today. A few years back we had a '50 years on' reunion in Enfield to celebrate fifty years since going up to Durham and meeting for the first time. No one had changed much at all and we simply took up chatting where we had left off as though it were yesterday.

That is the mark of true friendship, founded in a common experience. In truth we came from a mix of backgrounds, some from well-heeled families, some from the working class ones, but back then it mattered not a jot. We were all in it together. Nowadays I reflect how very privileged we were to attend such a prestigious university, run on a collegiate system along the lines of Oxford and Cambridge. Gaining a degree from Durham was an amazing achievement which unlocked for us many doors in life.

Nowadays I note when revisiting the city that it has grown exponentially and many of the traditions which marked it out – such as wearing gowns to dinner and lectures – have been disbanded. Students prefer their own rooms and the newly built accommodation caters for this. In my first year as an undergraduate we shared three or four to a room in Shincliffe Hall and thought nothing of it. Rooms may have had a washbasin but that was all. Kitchen and bathing facilities were more spartan and communal in nature. Yet I am convinced we benefitted from living closely together, learning tolerance and respect for others.

St Cuthbert's Society Durham university friends annual reunion, together on the beach at Bamburgh Castle (I'm second from the right)

St Aidan's College Durham University friends celebrating 50+ years of friendship, enjoying a posh afternoon tea at a London hotel. (From left: Jenny, Maggie, me, Cathy and Heather)

'Vorsprung Durch Technik/ Progress Through Technology': My Year In Germany

As part of my Honours German degree course I had to spend a year in Germany working as an English Assistant in a secondary school. It was a year of revelations! I was sent to Speyer, a small town on the banks of the Rhine not far from Heidelberg in the Rhineland Palatinate. I was able to make extra money by giving *Nachhilfestunden* (extra help lessons) to pupils and adults.

My most memorable student was a lovely gentleman who wanted to practise his English. He owned a porcelain factory and lived in a tasteful house, immaculately kept by an efficient housekeeper. He invited me to lunch before our lessons and encouraged me to order whatever I fancied from his housekeeper. The following poem tells of our beautiful friendship and how we complemented each other.

Vorsprung Durch Technik

Glossary:
Herr Ypsilon – Mr Y, from the title of a German romantic novel *(Ein gewisser Herr Ypsilon* by Barbara Noack, published in 1961)

I smile as I climb into his sleek Mercedes sports car.
In my head I am Isadora Duncan (minus scarf)
Lunch is whatever I fancy, he says.

His house is that of a typical German Bürger,
impeccably kept, tidy, unpretentious.
I see from the numerous crammed bookcases
that he is a well-educated retiree, keen on the Arts
but fun-loving too, cue the witty cartoon drawings.
We are practising English Conversation, for which
I am well paid. He asks the English for *Vorsprung*.
Progress, I say. And yes, he is indeed making
excellent strides with vocabulary and idiom.

He turns to me and smiles that beguiling smile,
ever the gentleman, humble, despite his wealth.
He owns a well-known porcelain factory –
fine china tea-services adorned with rosebuds
to grace the dining tables of the discerning.
As a newbie in a small provincial town
suspicious of strangers, he is helping me settle in.
Net curtains twitch as I alight from his Coupé,
coyly adjusting my Mary Quant mini-skirt.
I guess their disapproval. *White knee-high boots,
shock horror! Who does this Fräulein think she is??*
Back then I took delight in causing a stir.

With the help of Herr Ypsilon I master the *Technik,*
the knack of charming them, fitting in.
Though years apart in age we each learn from the other.
That year was undoubtedly one of the best of my youth!
Indeed it could be described as *Vorsprung durch Technik*

My Year at Cambridge University, Trinity College Choir and the Magic of Madrigals

Following graduation from Durham I decided teaching might be a good career to pursue. At that time it was actually better paid than jobs in science or business. I had really wanted to be a translator or interpreter but back then it would have meant a further two years studying abroad and I had already done a four year degree course and was keen to get earning. I was offered a place at Cambridge University to study for a PGCE (teaching qualification), as had one of my Durham friends, so we decided to share a flat together rather than go into a hall of residence again.

What a year it was! I was there at the same time as Prince Charles and regularly saw him cycling around, books under his arm. His college, Trinity, were looking for female singers for the choir and I signed up. End of term saw us singing Gaudeamus Igitur from the balcony in the great hall, while down below Prince Charles played his cello in the orchestra.

The highlights of my time there were many, including the May Ball and climbing into the Trinity College Master's private garden at night to play sardines with fellow students(!).

The best, however, was meeting Nicole Crossley-Holland, wife of the composer Peter Crossley-Holland and being picked for a madrigal quartet to sing for the Czech Ambassador in the London Embassy.

Nicole had brought to light an old madrigal in Czechoslovakia (as it was then) and had been invited to arrange it and perform it for his Excellency. What a thrill it was to attend the reception and sing for him! I think I must have felt rather overwhelmed by the occasion as the details of it are hazy now. I do remember wearing a very short little black mini dress with a huge white peter pan frilled collar. Those were the days of Mary Quant, Courrèges and the miniskirt, Biba and Bus Stop boutiques along the King's Road Chelsea. I thought I was the bees knees in my chic, sexy outfits! Wigs were also 'in' and I bought a long dark blond one on an Alice-band which I wore when going out somewhere special.

The academic year flew by. I somehow passed the final exams and was deemed fit to teach. That's when reality kicked in and I had to apply for my first teaching post. I didn't want to return to Lincolnshire, preferring to spend time somewhere more exciting.

The place to be was London in the sixties and I was successful in obtaining a post at a prestigious girls' grammar school in Croydon (Outer London). It was one of the schools belonging to the Girls Day School Trust, known in my time as The Girls Public Day School Trust, the leading family of independent girls' schools. They were fee-paying but with bursaries and scholarships for girls from families with limited means or possessing outstanding academic talent.

It was an amazing place to hone my skills, even if somewhat sheltered from the realities of the teaching world beyond the gates in state comprehensive schools!

The buildings were luxurious, facilities for staff excellent. The terms were shorter than in state schools and the pay a higher grade, plus Outer London weighting. I had landed in a place of great privilege. Teachers from the school were treated with great deference by parents and public alike – a far cry from the present day.

So began a career which I loved and which afforded me a good standard of living. Fate had indeed dealt me a great hand.

*My best friend Judith with her bridesmaids
(I'm on the far left)*

Arrival of the Queen of Sheba

Memories of my best friend's Cleethorpes wedding

Late July and we're waiting in the porch,
bridesmaids nervously clutching bouquets,

fidgeting with our stiff brocade dresses –
(I'm probably over-thinking my role,

more anxious for my best friend on her
wedding day than I am for myself)

Will it be different now, changed priorities?
I bite my lip, hoping our friendship will survive

Her white stiletto heels click clack on the tiles
like the ticking of a self-important clock

A midge zooms by and lands square on my nose
I sneeze loudly and everyone giggles out loud

We're listening out for the Queen of Sheba,
not the actual one, of course, the music from Aida

It's the signal to start processing down the aisle …
but none of us can remember how it goes!

So much angst whirling round in my brain
Will I too find the love of my life? What if I don't?

My train of pessimistic thought is broken
by a sequence of rousing chords from the organ

Is this The Queen of Sheba? Probably.
So for better or worse, down the aisle we lurch

like dodgem cars suddenly switched on,
nervously bumping into one another

This is it now, no turning back.
Let the nuptials begin!

At a church Summer Garden Party with Judith in 1952. My character was Little Miss Muffet and Judith's was Mary Mary Quite Contrary.

*Dressed as drummer girls at a church
Summer Garden Party*

Twenty Years On

Remembering my best friend Judith

We always wore matching outfits,
Judith and I
We could have been twins; sisters at least,
September babies, two days apart
born in the local Maternity Home.
Our mothers were actually best friends too,
My mum Kathleen and hers Grace

'All Things Bright and Beautiful' dresses –
That's what we wore on summer days,
Judith and I
They even had matching knickers too!
Wearing them we were true princesses
playing hopscotch under the sun.
(For in childhood the sun shone all summer long
or maybe that was that just how it seemed?)

We both had musical teddies for Christmas,
Judith and I
Hers long and lean and mine short and plump
Her bear looked an awful lot like me
As I was tall and skinny back then.
But my stout bear resembled her
shorter than me, more flesh on her bones

Saturday mornings brought weekend club
For Judith and I
Of course we had no TV to watch
no iPads or Playstations way back then.
We had to keep ourselves occupied
so we told each other make-believe tales,
did painting by numbers or played on the swing

We walked together to school each day,
Judith and I
Wearing the same blue macs with hoods,
white ankle socks, Clarks t-bar shoes.
Our hairdresser couldn't do trendy cuts,
She really only had one style she knew.
So both of us sported the same prim bobs
adorned with cute silk bows on top

During the six-week holidays
we'd skip together down Hardy's Lane,
Judith and I
Hand in hand, teddies under our arms.
we visited Billy the Bull on the farm
dared each other to climb on his pen
and tickle his back with mare's tail grass

At grammar school we were in different forms,
Judith and I
We both took A levels, Latin as well
Horace Odes and Tacitus too.
Boring, I thought, but she loved it to bits.
Due to a shortage of classroom space
lessons were held in the stationery store
perched side by side on crates of books!

At nineteen we both went to study at uni,
Judith and I,
same college, but with different friends.
Afterwards moved into teaching careers
history for her, languages for me.
She then returned to our old grammar school
but I was looking for pastures new
and took up a post in the London sprawl

She married first – and as you'd expect
I was Chief Bridesmaid, in blue brocade.
Naturally she was my Matron of Honour
in floral pink lawn with a rosebud tiara.
The receptions we had were identical too
for Judith and I
From memory I think we had chicken supreme
and Charlotte Rousse with Chantilly cream
(Well, whatever the trendy thing was at the time!)

Even when we were living apart
we always made sure that we kept in touch,
Judith and I.
Each time I had news, whether good or bad,
I would rush to the phone to call her up,
hear her say 'North Kelsey 490' …
Sadly cancer took her away,
her loss was incredibly hard to bear
But nothing can ever erase from my heart
that precious friendship which we shared.

Judith, I still want to rush to the phone
To hear you say 'North Kelsey 490',
but then I remember you're no longer here,
life has moved on and the whole world has changed.
I wish I had told you how cherished you were …
Twenty years on I still miss you so much!

With my mum and dad, aged 20

Teetotalism

Although my parents disapproved of the pledge being signed at six years old, my father never ever drank a drop of alcohol in his life, despite having been in the army in the war. He proudly told stories of how he resisted the demon in the face of provocation but turned a blind eye to my hints at boozy parties at university and was astute enough to realise that I enjoyed the occasional drink when away from home.

My parents did move with the times and actually allowed wine at my wedding some years later but drank none themselves. The final irony for my dad was the circumstances of his sudden death. At Halloween he had visited me and his grandchildren for the day with his sister Jessie. All seemed fine that day and he had driven off promising to visit again before Christmas. Only an hour or so later a policeman arrived at the front door, bringing the dreadful news that my father had died on the way home. He had suffered an aneurysm at the wheel of the car, which had rolled backwards downhill and crashed into the wall of The Ship public house.

The headline in the Grimsby Evening Telegraph next day read 'Local resident Mr Edmund Browning was found dead in a pub car park yesterday'!

Soon my telephone was buzzing with incredulous

members of Mill Road Methodist church enquiring whether this could possibly be true? How had Eddie come to be in a pub at all? Looking back now I can appreciate the irony of it!

My mother had died some years earlier. Afterwards, my dad was very lonely living alone in his bungalow. My mum had kept house, cooked, washed, baked, in fact done everything single-handed. He was like a lost lamb. By this time I was married and living away but moved up with my second husband to live closer, so that we could more easily drive the fifty or so miles to Cleethorpes at a weekend. Sometimes I would pre-cook a casserole and heat it up for Sunday lunch at his house. One of my favourite dishes was beef carbonade, which was made with Newcastle Brown ale. Reheated it was truly scrumptious and my dad really tucked in, savouring every mouthful.

'How did you make this?' he asked and I began my detailed instructions.

When I came to the bit about the brown ale, my husband suddenly gave me a sharp kick on the ankle under the table. I paused in mid flow and frowned at him, naively unaware that the casserole contained an unmentionable ingredient. Hastily my husband finished the list for me …

'It's got Bovril in it, malt extract. That gives it the flavour!' he explained.

'Well, whatever you've used, it tastes wonderful,' said my dad.

Hope is a Rainbow

Remembering my father's sudden death

They appear in the sky as if by magic,
harmonic cadences sweeping to earth
like ballerinas touching their toes

Fickle in nature, there one moment
then gone without trace, leaving a sadness.
As a child I knew they were special

I would pause to shield my eyes
and stare at the miracle unfolding –
each shaft of colour speaking its own wisdom.

Their visits were never random,
they came exactly when needed,
delivering a personalised message

Only later in life did full insight come –
an epiphany on a grey morning of despair;
bringing a message of hope in my grief.

Halloween … My father's untimely death …
A policeman at the door telling me to sit down …
A million questions whirling round in my brain

Why him? Why this? *Why now?*

In a nanosecond my life fell apart.
I could not contemplate life without him.
I drove to Cleethorpes, tears blurring my vision
Alone, so very alone!

And then a miracle … a rainbow overhead,
double arc, enfolding the raw grief,
melting away the blind panic. I suddenly knew
all would be well.

And so it has been ever since that day,
when in despair a rainbow has appeared,
its colourful arc bringing hope and reassurance

I am not alone. The rainbow is my guardian angel.

The Time Thief

You might say they were short changed,
my Mum and my Nan,

not much for his short life
snuffed out on the battlefield:

a clarinet – *did he ever play it?*
rosary beads – *did he turn to religion?*

I struggle to pull up an image of him;
broken like a china doll, faceless,

laid out in a foreign morgue.
Cannon fodder, that's what they were,

those Lincolnshire Regiment lads,
expendable. A guiltless sacrifice

Let's not romanticise the carnage with
images of poppies. Let's tell it how it was

He left not only a widow, but a toddler too,
my mum, their lives put on hold.

Nan eked out her widow's lot
by taking in lodgers

yet it was still not enough to buy
a grammar school uniform for my mum …

In the end just a clarinet
and a string of rosary beads,

but I never once heard them complain.
I took over ownership of his things,

kept them safe with his photo and medals
Not much to show for his sacrifice

Looking back I realise now
my early years were coloured

by their stoicism – it is
from them I learned my *carpe diem* attitude

The Verdict

They wake in shadow …
For them no brightness of day
no lavender twilight
Life stood still a century ago
for those young men
snuffed out in the stink of battle,
buried beneath a much-vaunted
blanket of trampled poppies

Far from home they were,
bereft of the comforting arms
of their loved ones,
hostages to fate.
Bravery and determination
shone out in the darkness,
beacons of hope in a world
steeped in grey

What would they tell us now,
those heroes?
Was it all worthwhile,
that ultimate sacrifice?

Or perhaps, observing
our 'progress' a century on,
they might deservedly
damn us with faint praise?

Nanny Buttle (left) with her sister Susanna Ekins

*The interior of the original Mill Road Methodist Church,
showing pulpit and choir stalls*

Cleethorpes: A Brief Overview

The town of Cleethorpes has been permanently occupied since the Danes arrived in the 6th century. Fishing was the original industry but it was subsequently developed into a seaside resort in the 19th century. Its expansion was greatly aided following the linking of the railway to industrial towns in Yorkshire.

Cleethorpes Pier opened in 1873 and the Promenade in 1865. Adverts proudly boasted *'five miles of golden sand'* and it became the go-to resort of day-trippers and vacationers from the Midlands and Yorkshire industrial towns.

It resisted attempts to be incorporated into the adjacent borough of Grimsby with its much larger population and renown as a major fishing port. In 1974, it became the Borough of Cleethorpes within the newly created County of Humberside (reverting, however, to Lincolnshire in 1996 when that county was abolished).

Interesting facts:
Cleethorpes lies on the Greenwich Meridian and its average annual rainfall is amongst the lowest in the British Isles. A signpost stands on the spot displaying distances to worldwide locations. North Pole 4,051 km (2,517 mi), South Pole 15,963 km (9,919 mi), New York City 5,602 km (3,481 mi), London 230 km (143 mi).

Local residents from Lincolnshire and the Humber area affectionately refer to the residents of Cleethorpes as Meggies; the two largest resorts on the Lincolnshire coast are known by their nicknames 'Meggies' (Cleethorpes) and 'Skeggy' (Skegness). Inhabitants born and raised in Lincolnshire are referred to as Yellowbellies, a term whose origins are widely disputed.

A Place to Grow Strong Bones

Glossary:
Pea-souper – thick fog, caused by the constant smoke from chimneys

Wind tousling my mane of curls, strands blowing between my teeth, making me retch

Toes numb in my boots like icicles chipped from the roofs of prehistoric caves

It shouldn't be as cold as this, you think; mind-numbing, skin-drenching ceaseless rain –

But it is! The East Coast bypasses the usual order of seasons; offering instead weather … which means

the sun needs a muffler, chilblains get lathered with sunscreen, in every pocket lurks an umbrella

doubling as a parasol, when fickle clouds have a change of heart. Men's hankies serve as mouth guards

when pea-soupers descend without warning. You need
a compass to find your way home, like a random game

of blind man's bluff. Yet no one bats an eyelid …
After all, this is Cleethorpes, facing out into the north sea

No guarantee that you'll laze on the beach,
even in high summer! The barometer is a cunning liar.

Oh the joys of the whimsical east coast weather,
keeping folk guessing … the climate's default position

Love Calls Me Home

A breath of cool air kisses my brow,
disturbs the tangled curls on the pillow.
The heady scent of opening lilies drifts up
from the garden.

Threads of childhood long ago
weave complex webs behind closed lids.
As the fuse catches and smoulders
the kaleidoscope shifts into focus

Floating through the open window
on a chill sea-breeze in late Spring
I sense invisible hands supporting me –
ghost hands, male and female

I watch myself on mornings of promise
wandering bare-foot along the beach,
catching the fishermen on the jetty, struggling
ashore with their haul of cockles and shrimps.

Clambering down the slipway to the
breakwater, I quietly stare out to Spurn point,
waiting for the revolving light to flash again,
for the incoming tide to fill the gullies

The film scene plays on in my head,
reliving that childhood magic,
my brain erasing negative scenes between
then and now, no second takes possible.

Startled, I wake again on the cool side of the bed
in sheets like shrouds. The silence is deafening.
Yet just for a tide-span I was there again,
back in that safe cocoon.

With pen in hand, aged 5

About the Author

Margaret Royall's passion for poetry began in early childhood. Retirement brought the opportunity to pursue her writing seriously, giving voice to acute experiences of loss, grief and chronic illness.

Margaret's first collection of poems *Fording The Stream* (2017) was published under the pen name Jessica De Guyat. Writing under her own name, she is the author of a micro chapbook (2019). She has been shortlisted for poetry prizes with *Crowvus* and *The Bangor Literary Journal* and her poems have appeared in various journals, anthologies and webzines.

Margaret is a member of several writing groups and performs regularly at Writers Live Southwell. She currently leads a Nottinghamshire women's poetry group.

Twitter: @RoyallMargaret

Website and blog:
greasleycottage.wordpress.com

Instagram: meggiepoet

Dedication

I dedicate this book to my much-loved family: My children, Simon, Holly and Alex Royall; My stepson Paul Royall, wife Helen and my step-grandchildren Sophie and Josef; My cousin John Ekins, wife Elsie and their family in the USA, Sean, Maggie, Penny and Enzo; My amazing school friends of 60+ years and their husbands/partners; Jackie and Graham Umpleby, Angela and David Pykett, Ken Howitt and Jeans Childs

Thank you to all of you for your love and friendship and for helping me to create this memoir.

Acknowledgements

I would like to thank all my writer friends who have encouraged me in this endeavour, especially my Iona Alumni friends and my tutors Angela Locke MA and David William Clemson, who have encouraged my talent, supported and inspired me and given me the confidence to believe in myself.

I would also like to thank Mark Davidson for his ongoing support and for choosing to include the following poems in several anthologies published by Hedgehog Poetry Press, of which he is editor: The Verdict, A Place to Grow Strong Bones and Vorsprung Durch Technik.

Special thanks also to my poet/photographer friend Gary Liggett for help with restoring some of the photos in the memoir and for his invaluable support and advice.

Finally thanks to Stuart Sizer, who provided me with historical information about Louth.

Printed in Great Britain
by Amazon